BRUNO GMÜNDER

RON LLOYD
BUILT!

CODY BROOKS

GENSCO
225 LBS.

KENJI

BLAINE SUMNER

MAC QUINTERO

ZEB ATLAS

MATT RYAN

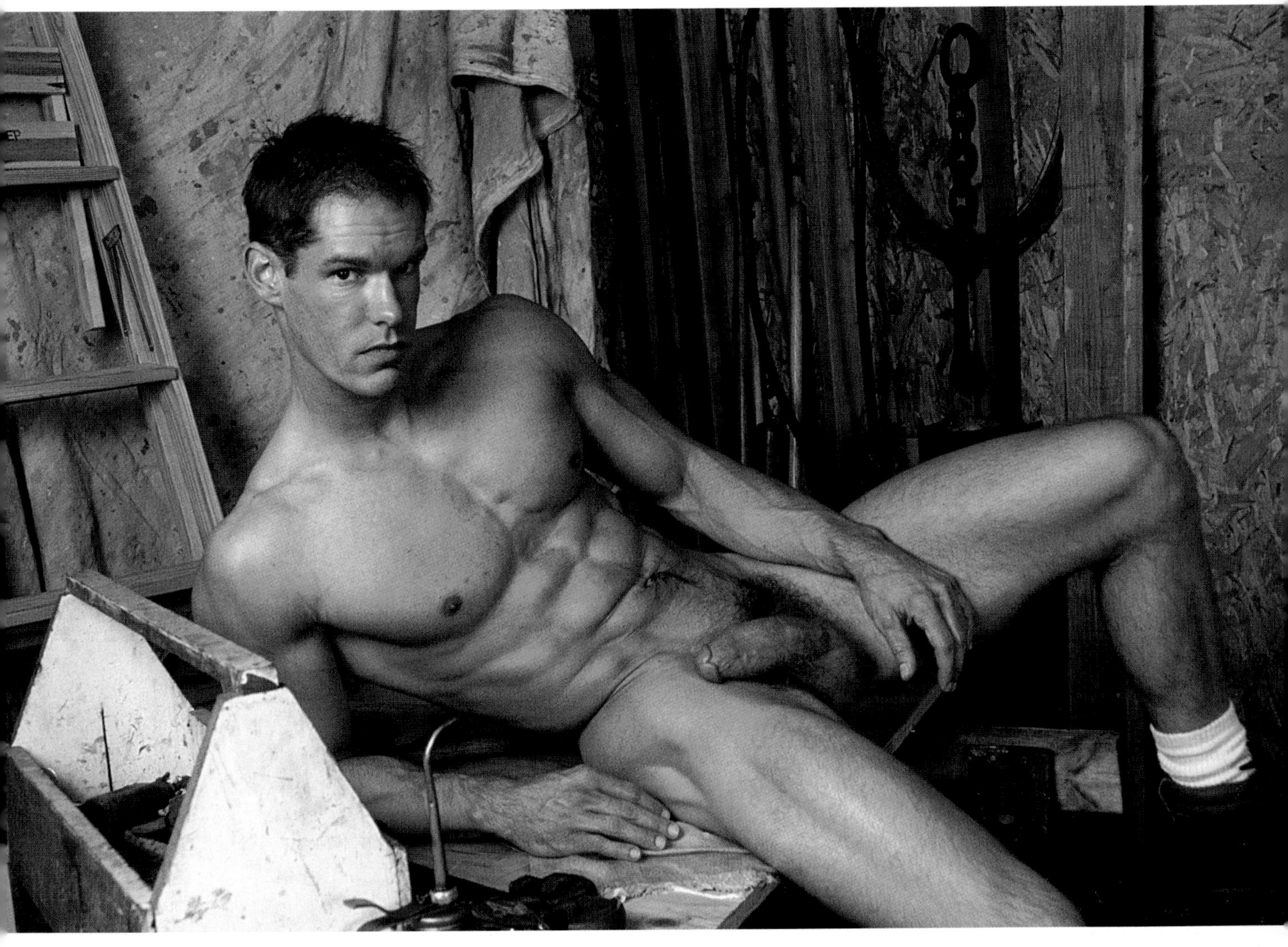

STEWART PARKER

CODY DALTON

SCOTCH

SAM DUKES

STEPHEN MITCHELL

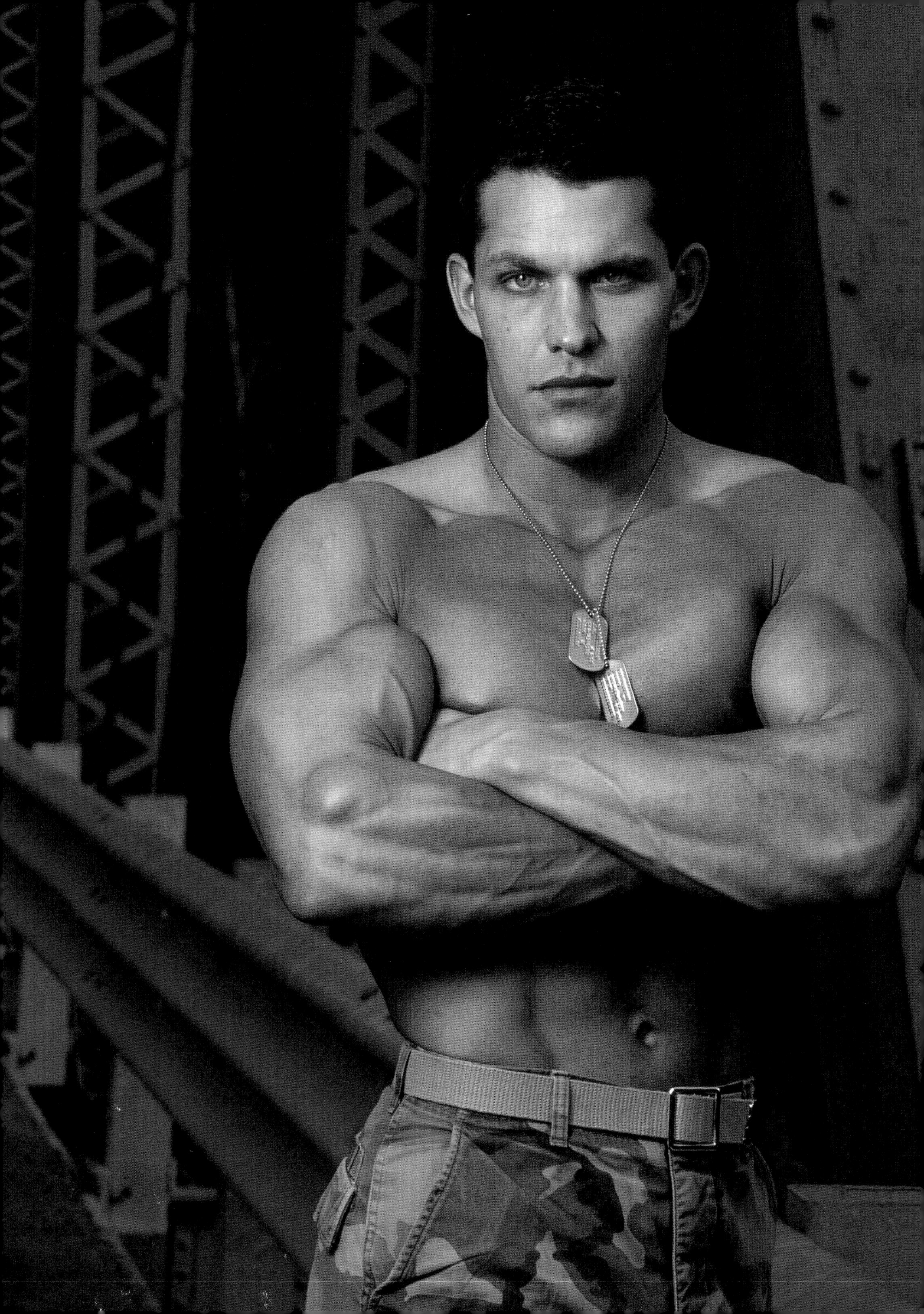

DANNY STEVENS

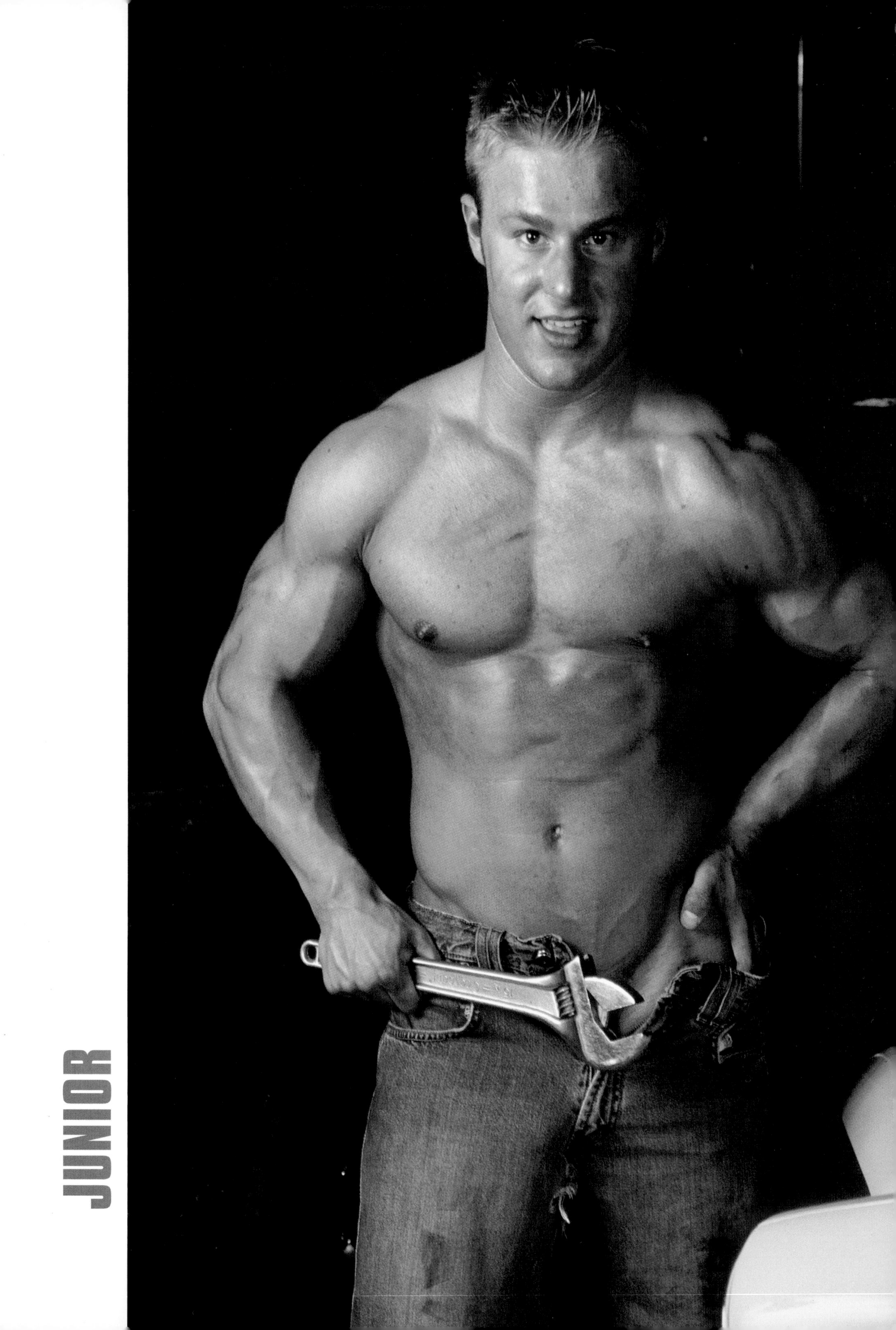

JUNIOR

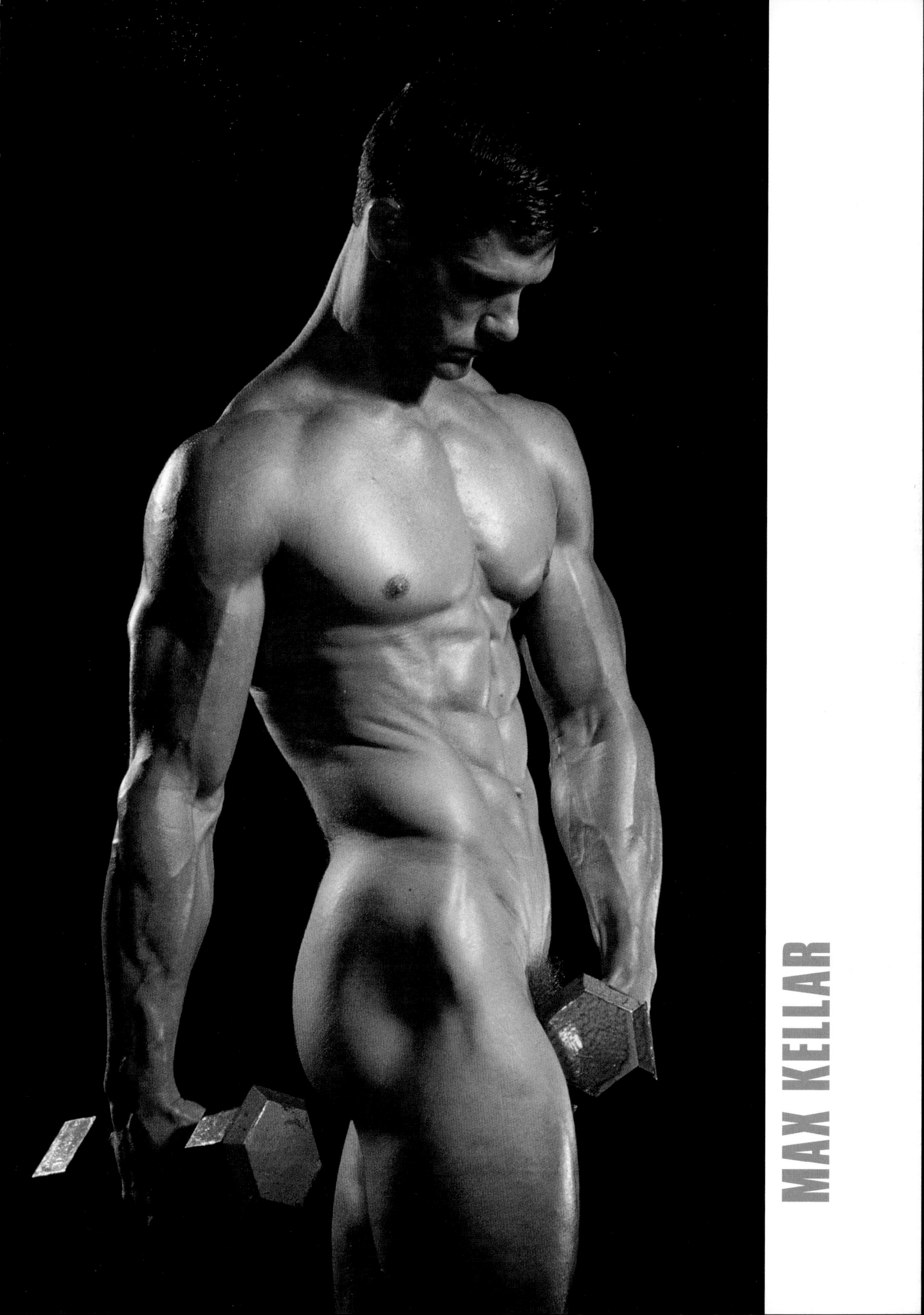

MAX KELLAR

NATE CHRISTIANSON

NATHAN BLACK

PRESTON SCOTT

RICK HENRY

ROBERT COLE

JAKE COLEBROOK

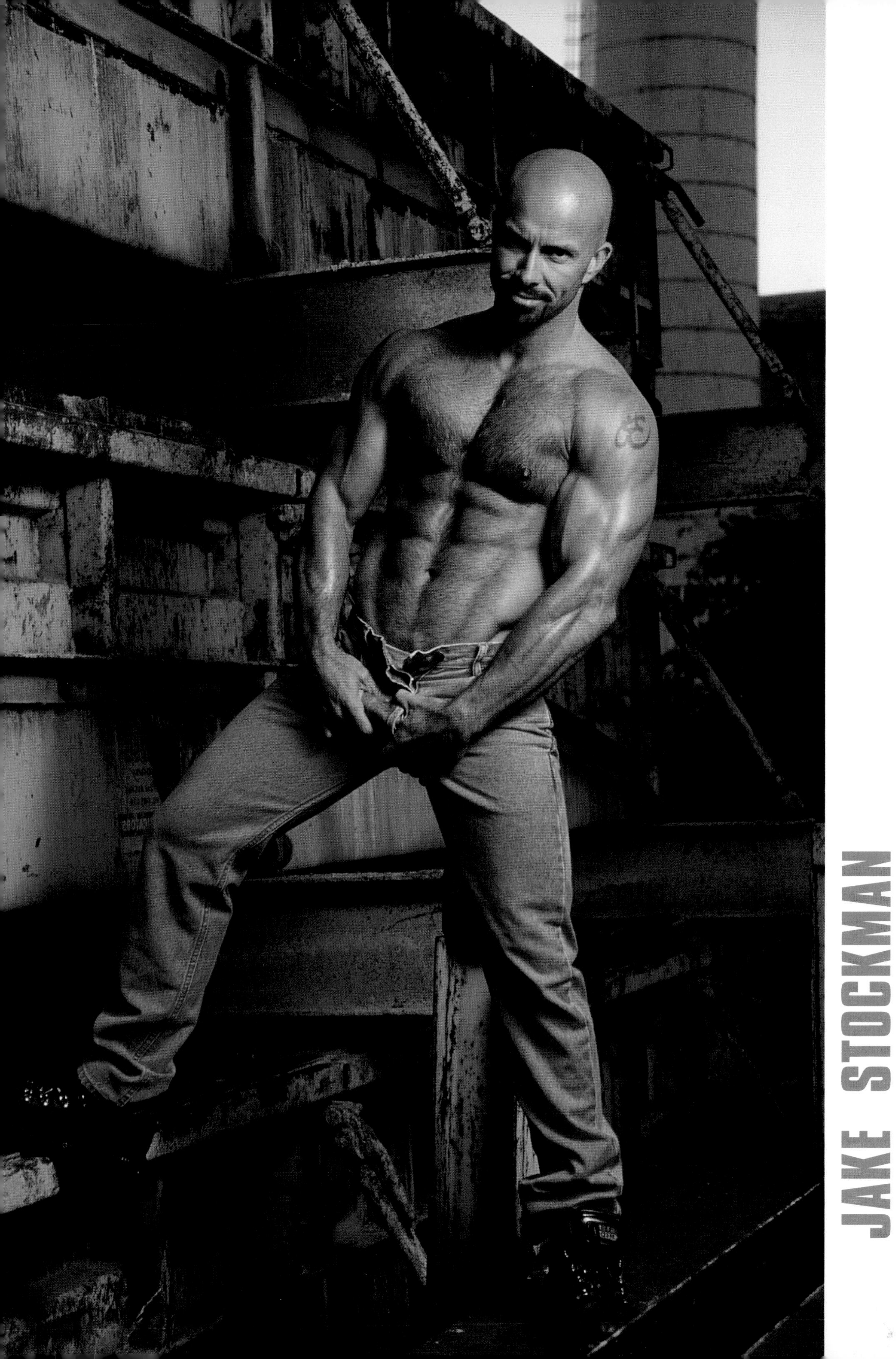

JAKE STOCKMAN

KONRAD BOLT

KURT ABERDEEN

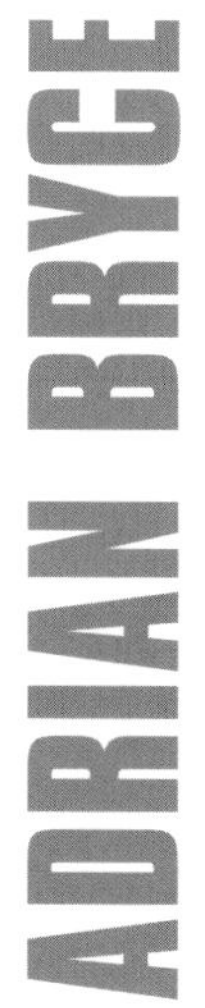
ADRIAN BRYCE

ANTONIO

CHRIS SPENCE

MARK JEFFRIES

ERIC

NICK RUSSO

VINCENT

ZANE

DARYL SCOTT

DON JACOBS

GUNNER

JOCKEY
JOCKEY
JOCKEY

Ron Lloyd acknowledged at a very young age his appreciation of the male form, growing-up in rural Pacific Northwest USA. He also was intrigued with cameras and the process of making an image. It was in college that he started working with male models for photographic assignments in the photography program in which he had immersed himself.

It was soon apparent that Lloyd's grasp of lighting techniques on the human form was an artistic gift.

After college, Lloyd started photographing competitive bodybuilders and other athletes to build his portfolio. During this period, Men magazine made it's debut on the newsstands and upon discovering the premier issue, Lloyd decided that he would someday like to do erotic photo-layouts.

A couple years later, Lloyd went to Los Angeles with his portfolio to meet the art director of Advocate Men magazine (now Men magazine). He left this meeting with his first erotic photo assignment. Lloyd did several shoots for Advocate Men and then decided to focus more on fine art photography.

In the mid-1990's he decided it was time to revisit the possibilities of creating erotic works for publication. Lloyd had instant success with the world of gay erotica under the name of Body Image Productions. He has introduced some of the most popular male erotic models in the last decade including Austin Wayne, Zeb Atlas, Vincent, Dick McKay, Nathan Black and Nate Christianson to name a few.

Lloyd continues to bring-to-light beautiful men in leading publications including Men, Freshmen, [2], Torso, Honcho, Mandate and Playgirl magazines. He is also crafting a video line featuring some of his most popular models with his company Body Image Productions. The Body Solo Series and Signature Series videos has captured an audience once limited to seeing Lloyds' work in print.

Acknowledgement

Thank you to Michael Taubenheim at Bruno Gmünder for his enthusiasm on this project. Caryn Goldberg at Specialty Publications for her commitment and support of my work.
Glen Offield, the first art director to give me a chance.
Mark Harvey, a former art director that truely believed in my work, and one who continues to be a friend and collaborator.
Doug McClemont, former publisher at Mavety Media Group.
And lastly, to my partner of seventeen years, Steve for his encouragement and love.

04 05 06 / 5 4 3 2 1

Kleiststr. 23-26 · 10787 Berlin
Germany
Phone: ++49 (30) 615 00 30
E-mail: info@brunogmuender.com

Edited & design by Claus Kiessling
Cover design & final artwork by Dolph Caesar
Printed in Italy

All models and characters portrayed are 18 years of age or older.

Parts of the photos courtesy Men magazine, Specialty Publications, LLC
Special thanks to Caryn Goldberg from SPLLC for the good cooperation.